LOVE, CRY

AND

WONDER WHY

By

BERNARD BRIGGS

Published by

Cauliay Publishing & Distribution

PO Box 12076
Aberdeen
AB16 9AL
www.cauliaypublishing.com

First Edition

ISBN 978-0-9554964-4-8

A CIP catalogue record for this book is available from the British Library.

For

Stephen

(13th December 1949 - 24th December 1949)

Forward

I was born and brought up in a village, just north of Chichester on the south coast of England. It was a quiet and fairly normal childhood in a small rural community, where everyone knew everyone else and life revolved around the church and the changing seasons. Looking back now it was pretty idyllic and it was in this environment that, in the early nineteen seventies, I started to write poetry.

Sometimes I'm asked what 'influences' my poetry and if I am, my usual answer is, 'me' and if asked what 'style' do I write in, my answer is quite simply, 'mine'! The thoughts and the words are mine, so to me it seems like a logical answer and I hope, not a rude one. That's not to say that occasionally my poems don't take on a recognisable style, but that's down to the poem rather than me, as they all have a life of their own; quite often turning out totally different from the original idea. The next question I'm asked is 'where do you get your ideas from'. That can be a bit more difficult to answer.

I remember as a young boy, playing in a large area of very long grass, just across the road from my family's house. Every summer, my friends and I would crawl around in the grass when it was at its tallest, creating 'roads' of flattened stems as we went. These 'roads' would, in turn, lead to 'rooms', where we would sit out of sight of any passing adults, playing a variety of games we'd invented, the rules of which are long gone. Alternatively, we might just lie on our backs looking up at the sky and talk about anything that came into our heads. The content of these conversations have, like the rules of our games, been lost in time. But it's a magical memory and one that sits alongside other memories, like walking home from church early on Christmas day morning, after midnight mass, just as snow started to fall, or on the same piece of road; saying goodbye to my first real girlfriend as we split up after the youth club disco. Over the years these memories have mixed with others from more recent times. For example, saying a final goodbye to my Dad at the undertaker's, following his death. The break up my first marriage; marrying my second wife, Mandy and watching our two sons grow up. Some of these are not everyone's idea of magical memories of course, but as we all know in life there is good magic and bad magic. I suppose that's where a lot of my poetry comes from; the experiences and memories that mark my life. Maybe the poems are markers in themselves; a record of me as a person and the people, places, situations and emotions I have encountered along the way.

Because the poems have their own identity and are sometimes quite personal and emotive in their perspective, some will be more comfortable to read than others. I often try to look for the less obvious view of things to try and provoke a response, but sometimes I like to look for the humour or absurdity in life, or the simple viewpoint of a child. As you read the poems, I hope you get to know them one by one and give them an understanding that means the most to you. In some ways, they are your poems now, so please feel free to find whatever emotion you need within them, but above all I hope you enjoy them.

A Corner of Time

An eye opens
From a corner of time
Brushes the world with light
Then closes

Tie your self to a dream, they say
Tight as a prayer
And drift as hope
On a butterfly breeze

I look at the blank page
There at my feet
I clasp at a thought; five finger tight
As a fragment of reason escapes me

The purpose is hidden by itself
A shadow with a shadow
Bite the dream then swallow
Float it up wondering, this or these

-o-

I stab the beasts
With bloodied spears
Until some life appears
Do not sleep now

An idea opens my breast
Run as fast as thread
You're a long time dead
Now do not sleep

A Falling for Him

Blood sprayed, splashed splattered
Skin ripped from flesh as wallpaper from a wall
Bone snapped, crunched, pierced muscle

-o-

A trip he had said
A trip to the coast
A lovely car ride through leafy lanes
Perhaps stop for a coffee at a café en route
Let's hope the weather's kind, but if it rains
Never mind
It'll be fun

Arrival is an anticlimax
There isn't much to see or do
Mist lies as icing on a cake
Wild flowers conceal their beauty
Grass
flops and
sags
The cliff top path is sharp and deadly

We pause on our walk
He turns
Our eyes enter each other

He's near the edge
His needs are reflected in the waves below
Crashing, surging, always advancing

A trip, he'd said
More like a trick

Hands grab my arms
Fear grabs my heart
Panic strips my sanity

I struggle, pushing
He gives way, slipping like
his
desire

Was he really waving goodbye
As he vanished over the edge

I was afraid
He was dead
I was glad, he was dead

A Fly

A fly

Flew onto the arm of the chair

How was it to know

That the hand which hovered there

Was

A murderer

A mortician

A coroner

A policeman

A lawyer

An undertaker

A coffin bearer

A priest

A gravedigger

A God

A Small Portion of Hate

I see a room within my mind.
An empty womb with a growing kind
of bubble. Something undefined.
But I fear it none the less.

The room is white; a jagged tooth.
A once smiled, cutting, piercing youth
of hurt. A distant truth.
A memory I'm keen to repress.

The bubble is silent; a floating bait
that lures me to an altered state
of being. A small portion of hate.
Long served, but still hot I confess.

I turn the handle and open the door,
step in and find a pin upon the floor
at my feet. A point without a law.
A balance I have to redress.

The membrane now dissolving fast,
the room is coloured red past
a care. Prepared at last.
A life without distress.

-o-

I invited you in and
we talked for hours.
You understood.
I understood
you.

A Thought

All life finds a meaning
So here I am, a part of you

Here with you
A small movement in time

Breathe me as the air each day and
Let me now give you life

Hear our hearts give melody together
A chorus of embraced lives

Our anthem is love
Sing

Alison Rainforest

I see you there before me,
all brave, without heart.
Lying still,
with eyes all pretending.
Reflective in salty wet questions.
Why, oh why, Alison Rainforest,
with all of its vision
does your mind
persist, as a blind fool;
stumbling in the light.

I see you there behind me,
hiding from yourself.
Lying still,
your face running with fears,
like a host of mistaken rivers
with no sea to run to.
You are remote, Alison Rainforest.
Deep, dark, damned to burn
in hopeless clouds of guilt.

Quiet now, come here and breathe softly.

I see you now beside me,
breaking away from the storm.
Lying still,
with that angel smooth smile.
One mile away from madness
and running.
Keep growing, Alison Rainforest.
Look behind you
just this once,
then wave goodbye.

All Things to All

I can be consciousness, honest and true,
Then be the liar, whose dark sky is blue.
I am the thought that knows only right,
Becoming the deed that belongs to the night.
Look, I'm the sunshine with all its warm days,
Just beware of the choir, with no voice to raise.
In all of the action that moves holy lands,
I am the devil, with time on his hands.

Whatever you want of me, evil or good,
I'll provide in an instant, like all servants should.
I'm in touch with your wishes, a mirror of black,
Just feed me with reasons and I'll be at your back.
A whispering killer of anger and love,
I'm a predatory hunter, a carnivorous dove.
Rely on my diligence, keep faith in trust,
Your freedom is a tether of barbed wire and dust.

In a life of obedience, I'm eager to please,
My tiredness is blinded by all that it sees.
My flesh is a martyr that no wish can save,
So foolish, so humble but never so brave.
As I lay down beside you, and melt to your form,
I am gentle and placid, the eye of a storm.
Believe me in all things, if risk is your game,
Only one truth is certain, the sound of my name.

Another Bad Book

Swinging the door on thickened hinges,
I turned and waited for you.
But in the permanent night of a turned out light,
there was a darkness we couldn't undo.
Stepping outside of our story
and reading it back to myself,
I discovered the truth had made love to the lies;
just another bad book on the shelf.

Another bad book lying dead on the shelf;
another sad story of need.
Another mad memory about fooling myself
into believing the things that I read.

Closing the door and turning the key,
was the saddest line on our page.
As I held your hand all the way down the path,
you were locking my heart in a cage.
Walking in opposite directions,
down a road with no name or desire.
Our lives turned a corner, on a new lonely course,
to a chapter more solo than choir.

Another bad book lying dead on the shelf;
another sad story of need.
Another mad memory about fooling myself
into believing the things that I read.

Turning the pages now; the story still hurts,
each word cutting deeper with time.
My memory slices each sentence in turn.
No reason, no sense and no rhyme.
Returning the book to its place in the past;
a dust covered history of pain.
I turn back the cover of an empty new love
and begin writing of hope once again.

Another bad book lying dead on the shelf;
another sad story of need.
Another mad memory about fooling myself
into believing the things that I read.

As One Life Ends

In a damp stale kitchen, quietly sit
Plate on lap; cup to lip
Eyes grow darker with each sharp sip
Shadows fill each black hollow pit

Heavy hearted drops of grime
Map out a trail of slippery slime
Down each pane, a watery mime
A reflective despair, an echo of time

Deep sigh in empty air, no light
As morning falls to afternoon's flight
Evening's clock gets tired of the fight
Gives up the ghost; no longer right

In a bed of rags, lay rigid and cold
Staring, gazing, no stars to behold
Drip down slowly in dreams of gold
Breath fading, passing to places untold

Float in a pool, a wish to stay
All pain and grief, dissolved away
Begin once more without delay
A long, long journey; let us pray

At Rest

Breezes ghosting tangled hair, bring
Faint wash of lives elsewhere
Roaring thoughts fade to a whine
As softly bells play soothing rhymes

Warming hands of dappled day
Smoothing limbs so rested lay
Sink slowly, gently, drift by dreams
Of no time, no place save here, it seems

Rising thoughts as eyes feel the light, of
Sharp cut images, oh so bright
Clear headed, stream like after rain
Spring to life and cooled, strong again

Balmedie Blues

Sitting alone on the dune,
my mind was out of tune.
Crashing the chords and
missing the notes I'd always struck before.
But then again,
the song had been written a long time ago.

The truth, like the sand
in my slowly closing hand
was hard to grasp.
The harder I squeezed,
the more facts drifted away
in the confusing breeze.

Why was this simplicity so hard,
and my weakness so easily scarred?
Creating all those twisted pictures
in my head had been a work of genius
and closing my eyes only kept out the searching
sand.
My sanity abstracted.

Black Bird in a Box

What shall I do?

Beat my wings
against the edge?
Turning me white,
shouting my name.
Or,
sit quietly in the dark.
But, then no-one will know
that I am the same.

What to do,
what to do.
I can't see a way out.

I'll close my eyes
and think about it
some more.

Black Ribbon

They sit in ill at ease ritual comfort
Redundant bookends with anarchic poses
The few words stacked between them
Unpacked from vanatised pages
A vacancy of sanitized phrases

Each scans the others lips for deaf ear truth
But they talk better than they read
Grasping the situation like their glasses of black ribbon
The catalytic clattering crap
That softens against the amber rocks

They dance with the poison from ignorance to bliss
Nothing has seemed as perfect as this
As foreplay it serves them only too well
But as evidence it passes them by
Then as time plays the killer
The ribbon
Unravels

Black Smudge Tumbles

Automatic billboard blinds
A parallel world
of portioned signs
The billowing paint
The dripping brush
From liquid canvas
to heartbeat hush
Counting tears
of stained glass rain
Flushed from heaving
clouds of pain
Wrenched to greeting
a cold suns rise
With interlocking
dreams and lies.

The black smudge tumbles
through a hundred mile sky
like jagged stabs
of nursery pie
Each feathery wound
Each flag whirling life
Mutates as treacle
when stirred with a knife
A dancer under a healing wing
that fails to notice
the sharp quill sting.

Blue Sky Over Snow

After the blanket had been thrown,
we drove
up into the hills
overlooking the valley.
Each bend of our journey bringing
gasps,
as the drifts got higher
and the road narrowed
to nothing but a wall.

Abandoning the car,
we walked.
Cracking the blanket
with damp sugar footsteps.
Animal tracks,
cool blue, under the sky.
Stalking their prey
in this February sigh.

Up by the bothy,
we stood
and blinked away the brightness.
Turning our heads, this way and that,
in an effort to believe
how smooth the land looked,

how tailored it was
to the field and road edges.
Tucked and pleated
into a bespoke jacket of crystal white silk.
Fragile, and cold.

Immobile, in our thoughtful dance,
we shivered.
The icy wind cutting us with its useless noise.
So, gathering our dreams with needle eyes
and silent mouths.
We slipped back into town,
along frothy brown streets.
Planning our cups
of warm sweet comfort.
Thinking of home.
Being home.

Body Language

Everyday he'd be there
at the corner, on his crate.
Facing the apathy, ignoring ignorance.
Telling it how it was;
how he saw the world.
His world.
Describing our fate;
destiny's gate.
On occasions, I would stop,
listening to his tirade.
But a while ago
I gave up the struggle.
So then, I just watched
him and those around.
That endless passing parade.
Watching, that was the education.
His performance merited an award,
as his eyes darted from left to right.
Arms raised, lowered, punching his point.
Twisting, pointing, fisting his palms.
His fears, doubts, anger outpoured.
Talk about multilingual body language.
No translation needed here;
no lessons.

This guy had passion, to pass on.
His oral message now lost,
war was declared.
As he pounded, expanded, gestured,
with an infantry of expressions.
In the small crowd one day,
another face, next to me.
I turned and whispered:
"Great isn't he?"
"Yeah, fantastic."
We smiled at our discovery.
Silently applauding.
Absorbing his actions,
discarding his words.

Times change.
Moving away from the town,
my world shifted elsewhere.
New life, fresh faces.
My animated orator was forgotten;
passing onto history's pages.

A year had gone,
before I returned to the past;
the futures birthplace.
Same streets, familiar faces.
Except that the corner
where a crate had been a stage;
where speech had danced each day,
was empty.

Devoid of any rush of blood.
"He died." The voice struck like a dagger.
The face from the past continued,
"Of gesticular cancer."
I smiled, sad as black.
Did he know what he was saying?
"Yeah, I watched him decline, almost overnight."
I imagined him wilting like a parched flower.
His proud bloom fading, falling.
The face disappeared,
into a diluted memory.
I stood quietly for a moment,
in remembrance,
then moved on.
This place held no power.

Boxes

Squared containers looking to hold our lives,
arrive skeletal flat packed and hungry.
Guts grumbling, greedily searching
for a feast of fleshy memories;
a bloated body of forgotten hopes.

Prowling in thoughtful chasms,
they gloat; made up mouths gaping.
Self important and impatient,
they wait for the feast.
Then all blinding teeth, they smash through the gate.

Multiplying, ever piling, whole beasts evolve.
Denting, then piercing vacant energies;
sucking us to dust.
Forget life, the muscle of dreams,
it pools around out feet, looking up for a light.

Bumble Sheep

The bleating, oh the bleating
of the stripy, woolly beast
As it buzzes through the undergrowth
always searching for a feast
With shearing teeth of razored bone
and a stinger on its rear
If you see it heading your way
let's get one thing crystal clear
The constantly ravenous Bumble Sheep
will strip you of your hair
Then peel your skin with dextrous ease
and a certain callous flair
After draining all of your juices
and portioning all of your flesh
It will devour your body totally
while your nice and fresh
The cuddly sounding Bumble Sheep
definitely isn't a cutie
It will eat you regardless of your looks
whether you're ugly or a beauty
But all's not lost for the human race
fearsome though this creature seems
Its range is somewhat limited
to your deepest, darkest dreams
So as you try to drift off late at night
and you resort to counting sheep
Just beware of the stripy jumpers
that may haunt you in your sleep.

Burning the Whole in Love

Love at the start, hate at the end
The time in between
Is torn, tattered and thatched with a need
Glazed with lies

The pattern emerges
Pain spikes an entrance
Maybe it's a vision
A dream draped in black

"Who needs this anyway?"
"How did this happen?"

Life's guests, in a whirl arrive
Peering at our lives
Trying to hide is a pitiful task
A mask, of sorts, obscures the truth

The reality is hard; scorching
Burning the whole in love
The whole bloody thing
A beacon for the damned

Cliff-hanger

Quiet and composed;
exposed on a ledge
between hard sky and soft earth,
the chisel wind howls,
deflected by an opening face.

Two million expectant years gone
and now just a pause away
from an atom of time.
The gasp of scorching breath,
that lasts for generations.

Engulfing grains of mountains pass
as pearly pin points.
Decoded sand, eroded and
resolutely driven by rivers of ice,
gradually release the teetering rock.

In time, all forces being unequal,
grip slips and casts
this new born into space.
Airborne once more; to soar
from the declining land.

While descending the face
towards deep blue eyes,
something ancient stirs quietly,
like a bee trapped, struggling,
inside its own honey.

The sandstone missile smiles knowingly;
spreads its drying wings
and speeds across the waves.
A mist of thoughts in creation;
evolution singing to the world.

Cloudy Monster
(September 2001)

Beware the cloudy monster and
grieve for our sons, the unknown army.
Cut down on the block of heaven's connection;
the concrete arms uplifted to God.
Brushed aside; crushed by suicide; homicide.

Beware the cloudy monster;
the slithering, dusty death,
that chokes the heart from innocent chests;
that strikes like a fist with silent anger,
then exhausted, covers whole worlds like a shroud.

Beware the cloudy monster.
Do not awaken or stir the beast
that moulds to the streets; the new world's pasture.
Tread carefully through its body to war.
Remember, from high or low, a fall is still a fall.

Beware the cloudy monster.
Its spawn hides deep within us, waiting.
Do not feed fear's offspring; starve its hope.
Go capture this moment in history's future.
Be brave
Be strong
Be love

Cold Resolve

Mud was the world
That and the silent, still puddles
Tinged with blood, that lay in
Pits of hoof and boot

Rigid and prone while battles talked
Back and forth, long into the night
Then cold resolve, steeled heart's ache
As dawn lit death at last

Dried splashed face of guilt
Upturned, in question's grip, to heaven
Paid the price of life that's given
Rose quietly, quite small, afraid to fall

Paced the return; the streets to salvation
To home, the memory's painted palace
Where reward could always be found
Where love never failed to breathe

and where dwelt warm, soft dreamy lies of
laughing children, clean and bright
bellies full against buckles tight
of a lasting peace, both day and night

But then despair; the cancer of hope
As the journey's weakened lungs expired
And knees met sod to pray
Hand clasped hand to beg

Darkness was the world
That, and hell's lullaby
The sound of booted, well oiled metal
Breath held, saved for God

Fire!

Commitment
(for Mandy)

I step forward,
leaving a mark on the land.
An imprint of hope,
that we both understand.
We've embarked on a journey
to a place in our hearts.
Where our souls join together
and eternity starts.
For a life spent in union,
is a vision we share.
An experience of loving;
of showing we care.
In this future, I promise
to be faithful and true.
My honest commitment,
to always love you.

Crop of Gold

Flat sunshine, stretched over soil
Deep heated, swaying gold
Patch here, patch there
Glowing against the green

Fools cry rape

Beautiful I cry

Daddy's Treat

On a tray:
Kitten tea
Tiger toast
A cereal offering
With spoon in brimming bowl

Borne by tender souls
Tendered in trembling hands

"Happy Father's day", they chorus
Both smiling at the bedside

Then they're gone
Dashing to catch up
As the final
Colourful
Moments pass

Dame Street

Dusk:

Dame Street bubbled under hot feet and wheels.
The arterial tar, pumping rubber and heels.
A heated discussion of colour and noise,
between a kissing of girls and a bashing of boys.
All shoving along in their earnest pursuit
of a fatal ambition, down a drinkable route.

Midnight:

Restaurants troubled by the hungry and drunk.
The traditional bars pumping fiddles and funk.
All vying for the euro in the crazy descent,
from tired tatty urban, to a classic lament.
Vanity paraded past convenience stores
and Friday night shadows, on crack opened doors.

Dawn:

Taxi rates doubled, chasing night into day.
The mother of stars pumping dust from the fray.
A memory of muscle, from the thrill of the chase,
with heads full of images, inhaled from this place.
On Dame Street the fragrance is heady not sour,
just dark thickened sweetness, of a Dublin street
flower.

Dancing Hair

My little lad
has dancing hair.
A style he's made his own.
It twists and twirls
from here to there
and has never met a comb.

But that's just him,
a bright wee thing,
with rules he sets - or not.
To obey, or change upon a whim,
a story with no plot.

So, dervish like
this mane so bright,
performs its hirsute ballet.
His choreographic, curled delight,
a soul and hair day tally.

Danger - Child at Thought

What is that man doing up there
and I wonder what he's thinking.
He keeps on smiling down at me,
perhaps he's been out drinking.

I'm only sitting in my pram,
watching the clouds drift by.
Oh dear, now he's making a funny face,
perhaps he's swallowed a fly.

It could be that it's cold up there
and the chill has gone to his brain.
Or maybe it's just that he's very old,
it must be such a strain.

Oh goodness me, he's coming down,
this could be scary Mummy.
But if he tries that coochy stuff,
I'll batter him with my dummy.

Danger Child at Thought -2
(Tangled Shadows)

No, don't get near me, can't you see it's sunny
I'm really, really sorry but I am not being funny
No, please don't come any closer, come around the other side
I'm not risking tangling shadows; it's a thing I can't abide
Once we tangle silhouettes it's curtains, so be careful please
Or our minds will become all jumbled up, like a jar of
coloured beads
I don't really care about the pavement cracks as my mum's
got plenty of pots
Just take care not to tread on my shadow; it's a thing that
worries me lots
Once it happens though, it's final; it's a terrible job to undo
We'll probably spend our lives entwined, in the shade, stuck
together by shadowy glue
So please keep well away from me when the sun is bright in
the sky
But on friendlier, overcast cloudy days, I'm not the slightest
bit shy
The danger zone is definitely when, unexpectedly, the sun
comes out
Then, if you're standing a little too close to me, your shins will
receive such a clout!

Diving Into my Sweatshirt

"Dive in", says Daddy
"Come on, in you get"
I outstretch my arms
Take aim and jump
But don't get the slightest bit wet

-

The 'pool' is my school sweatshirt
It's much, much bigger than me
Mum says that I'll grow into it
Yes Mum, when I'm about twenty three

I do a few laps in the inky depths
Trying to find what's about
Somewhere in here are three big holes
For my arms and my head to stick out

It's a difficult business, this getting dressed
When your clothes are like the Pacific
And you swim around for hours at a time
It's a pain, to be really specific

But then…
Deep in the gloom, I discover a moon
Three planets, some stars and a rocket
A pirate ship and a giant whale
Lurking just behind a breast pocket

Caught up in a fold, I uncover some gold
A football, a bike and a scooter
I fight with a shark and a dog with a bark
And I thump a T-Rex on the hooter

Rounding a kink, in an armpit, I think
I spy a monster with a frightening head
As it gets closer and scarier, I realise now
It's actually my daddy instead

That's it then, I'm near to the surface now
And I'm coming up for some air
I suppose I've delayed things enough now
It's time to fight a war with my hair

Does every child in the world go through this
Or, am I strangely unique in this way
Taking hours to getting ready each morning
As I confuse getting dressed with just play

Doubts About Sanity

My dark brain offers a hand,
still, it's what they would want.
Now and then, a glimmer of truth appears
which is soon lost in a tangle of thoughts.
The right thing to do is the main objective,
but is it correct to pander to popularity?

My crooked mouth utters politeness,
but what I mean to say is no longer there.
Someone, somewhere has my words
and using them strikes me dumb.
If only I could say what I think,
instead of trying to win a smile.

My hands do as I bid; they are trustworthy instruments.
Legs, arms, feet, act according to instructions.
The instructions are to blame though I think,
but then, a sick workman always blames the rules.
Control of the elements is the difficulty here;
they spin and weave, never making headway.
One day they will crash and die!

Drifting Off?

Tired as a stagnant pool
of forgotten raindrops, I lay.
Listening to the rush of blood;
the course of life flow by.

Muttered voices drift along, laughing
and I yearn to know the reason why or what.
How do they live without me?

I'm suddenly aware of my skin,
A case for the soul
Do I match; do I tally?
Does my mind balance the scales?

Dim darkness rescues further thoughts,
as sleep descends once more.

Fall and Fall

First rush of blood:

Your heart recognized me
As I floated
face down in myself;
clutching at the world
with a baited smile

Your eyes invited me
Beautifully engaging mine
in a graceful conversation of looks
A home fire flickered at last in the dark,
as I passed my heart into the glow

Your tongue received me
Passionate and probing;
wrapping me in a tartan shawl
I sighed, but could do nothing at all,
but fall and fall and fall

Your body entertained me
It entertained us both
stroking and bending
us into our favourite secrets
Two rhythms pulsing toward one life

Realization:

You have given me everything
A heart to cry with
a soul to love with
a smile to reply with
a reason to live
a future

Can I give you my love
It is all that I have
but I give it wholly
Now
and
then
again
and
again

Fall Asleep

I fall asleep
into unfinished dreams,
with bible story skies
and long greetings
between the sea and its shore.
Into memories I'll lose;
fallen comrades in war.

I fall asleep
into unfulfilled hopes
with fairy story lies
and fractured farewells
between the body and its soul.
Into memories I'll miss;
an old actor's new role.

I fall asleep

Fear

Show me a light that burns forever
and I shall defend you the dark places.
But I fear that the whole is too big;
it swallows all that should be reflected.

Show me the face that sings of hope
and I shall strengthen that hope with wisdom.
But I fear that doubt has too deep a root;
it will not die on receipt of a smile.

Show me a colour that dances alone
and I shall cause a palette of drums.
But I fear that no rhythm can paint such a beat;
while time marches on, sliding into final muted tones.

Show me a word that has love in its heart
and I shall read it with love in mine.
But I fear that no language can cry true tears;
merely cast a shadow across dreams and destinies

Finale

In the night
She cannot see
The look of indecision on my face

We walk the straight
Then turn to the narrow
We stop

I open my mouth to speak, but
Only lies escape
Once innocent lips

Water flows from eyes
Rivers on a dessert
Welcome, but hopeless

Silence; doubt; regret
A chorus line of emotions
All vying for the light

Later we stand in the road
Kiss cheerio
Then, opposing poles, we part

Curtain

Forms in the Sand

Through changing light,
the crystal twists.
Creating moods and forming lists.
Absorbing, reflecting
my altering states.
The encrypted message
of facets and shapes.
Though chained to my being
with sinuous steel,
its feathery touch is easy to feel.
As refractions encounter
each beam shining through.
I bend to the task
of mirroring you.
In your hollows of hope
and spiralling dreams,
I am your companion in colouring themes.
We fall into rainbows
and dance in our skin.
Watching the magnified
visions begin.
Now lightening defuses
our forms in the sand,
evolving new gems from this wind sculptured land.
A fusion of elements,
into crystalline forms.
A protection, a sanctuary,
in gathering storms.

From the Dark

Shame we cry, as nothing changes;
as a pure idea is drowned in doubt.
Drain our heads of hope and dreams,
then pierce our eyes with grand designs.

Gather a grey dawn, break out the colour,
display in the sun, lay it bare, prone, stark.
Open our eyes now, our minds and our hearts,
help us, lead us stumbling from the dark.

Good Grief
(Are there cakes in heaven?)

Black, a sea of black
In mind, on body
Hanging in the air, draped
Around lives bitten, attacked

Motion is muted, reserved
Eyes dipped in purple, stare
At stony, tortured faces
Gripping onto a love dissolved

Mumbles whisper all the while
Of brighter days
Viewed through a sunset haze
Death though, refuses to smile

'What have we got to live for
This life has no meaning at all
We're born, we die
No one remembers where we lie'

'Good grief, is there such a thing
Do we reach a place
Where God is guaranteed
When we know he's listening'

In the centre of it all
The brightest despair
A crumpled figure
Once so tall
Raises up a question's eye
Her thoughts needing an answer
Her pain needing a reply
A mother needing a son

"Do they have cakes in heaven?"
The words sting
"He loved his cakes, you see
So, do you think there are cakes in heaven?"

-o-

Everyone agrees, there must be
A cake or two up there
Plates full of fondant fancies
And creamy gateaux to share

At once the mood is lifted
Everyone's discussing the idea
That there must be a patisserie in heaven
Making pastries for our departed, so dear

A flick of s switch and there's music
Meandering around the room, touching hearts
The mumbling, gloomy talk of death
Turns to Battenberg, cream and jam tarts

It's a positive feast of remembrance
A joyous celebration of life
Of the things our loved ones enjoyed the most
Like the surrender of a flan to a knife

A foot taps quietly to the beat beat beating
Of a tune that has meaning; has soul
And the shroud is carefully discarded
With tales of éclairs eaten whole

Raising the roof with warm memories
grabbing hold of the stars, clutching tight
Are there really cakes in heaven *(I hope so)*
Not sickly, not sugary…just right!

-o-

Colours, like oiled water, dance
Merging, twisting, diluting sorrow
Fading slowly to clear emotion
Happy that life continues, infinite

Goodbye

So, our journey together ends.
You, walking away
from my outstretched hand.
Me, clutching at the cold air
with a falling heart.

'Ground Force' Day

Chop chopping choppery whack
Sawing buzzily creaking crack
Rake readily wearily ruffle
Borrowed wheelbarrow push with a shuffle

Clip clippy clippery snap
Hack happily hackery slap
Brush briskly sweepily clean
Tidiest spinney there's ever been

Shred shredder shuddery crunch
Branchy breakfast leafy lunch
Weed willingly weedily swish
'tis a dappily shadowy place we wish

Tyred tired tiredly trudge
Fingernail dirt that just won't budge
Home foamily lazily bath
Enough grit in our ears to lay a new path

Learn learning learnery nook
Play playfully head in a book
Cool cooling relax in the shade
'til next time the ground force returns with its spade

its fork
        its rake
                its shears
                        its broom
                                its shredder
                                        its chainsaw...

Haiku

Gold and black gliding
Over indescribable
Liquid and solid

-o-

Resting after lunch
Abnormal things go on around you
But go unnoticed in your dreams

Heart With Attitude

He has the biggest heart I know
My little bundle of life named Joe
"I've got heart with attitude"
He once said to me
So honest, so true, so matter of fact
Like saying what he wanted for tea

Hope Embrace

Embrace me now
under a painted temple sky.
Quiet and
respectful.
Resplendent,
before a witness of waves.
Eager to see our love,
marry the sand; melt
into the world.

Can my dreams wait?
Can I can touch your
lips with a thought
and feel your breath
mix with my breath?
I am stirred by a word,
so softly spoken, it hangs,
on a single beat of
silence.

Your name then appears
in the palm of my hand;
drawn there by a wish.
It smiles as always,
before joining the air.
Together, we watch it fly.
Carrying our dreams.
Into a cloudy window
of regret and hope.

Horrible Hans

Hands gripping an elegant throat,
squeeze the pulse beneath milky skin.
Admiring the performance, his tools work so well,
look so good. Drop a smile, a gloat.

Remembering this deed as those before
will pleasure him on the quiet calm nights, when
temptation is dormant, rekindling its force.
To lead again through evil's door.

The job in hand though has needs of its own,
to distance him from this deed, as
flesh departs this physical world, to join
the sawn and broken bloodied bone.

Task complete, home to a bed of
tacky blankets, grey crumpled sheets
in a room so stark, so empty, so
dark, not one single light is shown.

Sleep then, 'til night time, a blanket of black
to cover, conceal the world from light.
Prepare, for the curtain, rehearse the finale.
Quietly, the make up, the tools of attack.

Now, lain like soldiers awaiting the call.
Select each hue, each textured weapon
and apply with love and caring attention.
Suitable paint to frighten and appal.

Clipped neatly, digital razors spread out wide,
to be filed and buffed, glossed and sealed. Then
blown upon with fowl, sweet breath.
Gazed upon with ghastly pride.

Beware then, of the manicured Hans Bojangle.
Be watchful on dark and lonely paths;
desperate, dilapidated, disposable places,
where necks will snap and sinews dangle.

Horrible Hans has manicured plans.
So, trust not a man with a grip of black satin
whose voice is sugar on make up and stuff.
Knowing women you see, he understands.

A demon; walking and working through death,
to snare and trap, envelop from life.
Meet the monster – meet thy maker.
"Hello, I'm Hans, draw your last breath."

If black had a dark side, like pitch, unlit
Hans would be it!

I Dreamed I Had Hope

They're here;
piles of leaves, out of season.
Haunting us;
sneering a dutiful reminder.
Where did our dreams go?
Discarded.
Each corner turned,
brings a fall of faith
into a familiar pit.
A trap, a trip.
Where did our hopes go?
Forgotten.
Clean, cleared wood
with naked wishes shining.
A journey's first beat
to honest ambition.
Where did our lives go?
Ignored.

Idea

I see a door in my head

Black as a throat

Squeezed to a strangled cry

Knock, then run away

I'm Here Waiting

Don't try to please them
It's easier to please me
Don't hold onto the past
I'm here waiting

No point walking the streets
Looking for someone
Who's not there anymore
I'm here waiting

Why worry about the future
When, without me it's not there
That's why
I'm here waiting

Love is something I know about
I've read it all in books
Now I'm ready and
I'm here waiting

My address is enclosed
My telephone number to
I know I only love you
So, I'm here waiting

I'm Not Phillis Wheatley

Should I be writing poetry, without an axe to grind?
I'm not underprivileged; not deaf, or dumb or blind.
I'm not a victim of savagery, of bigotry, or hate.
I'm only clinging to a hinge of words, on a wildly swinging
gate.
It's a five bar hurdle to a field of corn, with a wilting crop of
rhyme.
Am I the farmer of barren land? Am I running out of time?

Should I be writing poetry, without hanging it on a cause?
Though breeding insecurity is worth a minutes pause.
No, my words should demand some justice, for any wrong
that's done.
Put my stanzas on a soapbox; arm my sextains with a gun!
A word without a meaning is like a tree without its root.
Just a wooden stick with not a hope, of ever bearing fruit.

Should I be writing poetry, without suffering in some way?
I'm not talking about my waistline here, or my patch of
thinning grey.
It's a fact I'll have to live with, a truth I'll have to face.
I've no first hand experience, of a persecuting race.
No, I'm not Phillis Wheatley, whose voice helped soothe her
pain.
Just a hopeful heart, with wordy blood, in search of love
again.

In Life

In life,
An eye beholds a vision
A word heals division
A thought holds a moment
An action shows the way

In life,
A feeling inspires a message
A doubt delays its passage
A pause reflects the meaning
An innocent kneels to pray

In life,
A heartbeat warms an embrace
A love remembers a face
A body touches a body
An image invited to stay

In life,
An opportunity needs direction
A voice demands reflection
A reason finds the question
A goodbye ends the day

Incommunicado

They perform
as separate entities.
Chucking shit at each other.
Plucking ideas from the air
on how not to conform.
Hard to believe
they survive.
Yet side by side
they scowl and connive.
Firing adjectives and nouns
as pointless vows.
Like arrows
in a fist fight.
Can I carry on veering
from elation to deflation,
impressive to depressive,
in this civil disobedience.
This war between want and need.

Can I say something
and mean it?
Can I feel something
and understand it?
Can I think of something
and remember it?
Can I love something
(and stay in love)?
Whilst my
mouth waters
as my
heart wrenches
as my
head aches
as my
soul searches.

I am incommunicado.

Just Checkin'

There he was beside me
Almost instantly
A flash of air and blonde hair
I hadn't seen him approaching
In his camouflage cargo pants

"Hello!" be boomed
Like a twig with the voice of a branch
"Hello," I offered down to him
Hoping he would go
Hoping my stare would throw
Him back to his Mum and Dad
But he looked at me with equal eyes and said

"Do you know how to hypnotise
a chicken?"

I didn't say I did and I didn't say I didn't
But he looked at my expression
Which really said it all

"Go on then, tell me."
I dared his smile to amaze
He met my gaze
"Well…"
His grin got eye powerful

"…paint a white line on the floor
and get the chicken to follow it."

A hopeful heart floated in the silence
I smiled
He smiled some more

"Why didn't I think of that,
it's so obvious."
He was oblivious

He just turned and ran off, shouting
"Just checkin'."

I began thinking
Of inebriated poultry and Paul McKenna

Let's Get Whispery

Let's get whispery
Not wispy or tipsy on whisky
Let's get in a huddle
Not a muddy muddle
Let's get closely, mostly
Don't get horse, get hush
Let's get whispery

Let's get whispery
Release a sacred secret
Let's get gossipy
Give me the low low down
On life and love
Let's get whispery

Let's get whispery
It's warm and inviting
To talk ancient history
May I steam up your ear
With a moment of misery
Or a memory or two, of lovely goo
Let's get whispery

Let's get whispery
Giggle he-he-hysterically
Chuffle incessantly
Tickle our funny bones
Bounce quiet words together
Let's get whispery

Let's get whispery
But enunciate crisply
Our love prose, slowly
Not too swiftly
Listen carefully, to the prayer, fully
It's intimate, clearly
Let's get whispery

Whispery

Live Eight

The party started
with a million deaths.
Oh, how we cried
at the diamond screen hosts,
and their three second lives.

The beating started
with a thoughtful pretence.
But as the flickering faces
smiled a hunger of teeth,
they still had no meat
for their knives.

Look of Love

Walking the streets,
staring straight ahead.
I meet the approaching eyes,
thinking the me.
Believing the I in my blindness.

I am afraid of the look
to left or right.
Through the windows
to other lives.
Into the doorways
of opposing thoughts.

I cannot see
the thoughts, or the lives
that give them life.
So I wander in the truth of
invisibility through ignorance.

I dream of
smiling acceptance.
I look, but not
really look.
I love, oh I really love,
but only others see.

Matriarch

We gathered the ghosts
of past souls around us.
Greeted them once more
and pledged remembrance.

We moved their names
into a distorted reflection.
Memories that pushed
the cold air through any sentence.

-o-

She was...

The centre of our circle
The axis of our years
A guiding light, a beacon
From laughter through to tears

The foundation of our future
The life producing spark
A safe and gathering pair of arms
To protect us from the dark

The constant in our being
The rootstock of our tree
A giver of unquestioning love
For all the world to see

-o-

We were a discussion of daffodils;
animated in the flickering snow.
Safe and warm within our walls
of darkened outer skins.

We steadied our fingers
over the switches, then stabbed!
Deathing the night; birthing the light
and without her, attended to our new futures.

Mind Over (doesn't) Matter

Free your mind, release the thought
That lurks and loiters in your head
Looking for a point; a path to meaning
Let loose the ideas that hide inside
Unfurl the banner of brightness and worth
Don't be afraid if it hurts, or if it's slow
Sometimes the flow, doesn't know where to go

Why worry when things go badly or black
The words like a good idea will always come back
It's not easy to relax and let your mind go blank
So just treat it like an account at the bank
Empty it quickly, use up the reserves
That'll ease the situation and settle your nerves

Put the pen to the paper, don't try and think hard
The pen will work wonders when you're not on your guard
Watch it flow freely; watch it move on the page
See how much time it takes, a minute, an age
So off you go now and create something grand
You'll be pleased with the result and it won't have been
planned

Misty Morning

Mist swirled and tasted the trees
as the grass, coated in tears, slept on.
The morning light was pale and tired; diluted.
A sun
surely not ours
hovered on the horizon,
then slowly climbed, painting the sky;
banishing the dusty shade.

No wind or noise lived here,
just a silent offering of thanks.

My Life the Field

Like a mirror's eye,
one raised sword
is matched by another,
as battle is joined.
My life the field

Still, as hearts poised
before a blow;
a cut foretold
by thoughts and dreams.
My life the field

Drawing the blood
releases the tirade.
The genetic mould,
though attacked, remains.
My life the field

Black or white,
no-one has a doubt that
the darkening sky
never brings the night.
My life the field

Secretly drawn up to the wall,
the enemies fight on;
a challenge uncompleted;
a lost cause to believe in.
My life the field.

My Little Sun's Tears

Why is my Sun so unhappy
Why is it not up there in the sky
Is it because the clouds have been angry all day
And they've made the little Sun cry

His tears fall through the swirling clouds
And he's no hanky to wipe his eyes on
No friend to cheer him up, no friends
To tell him there's nothing wrong

The crashing thunder frightens me
It sure must be worse way up there
The lightening flashes and dashes around
I hope the Sun knows that I care

When the suns not out, we all feel sad
Gloomy certainly isn't fun
So lets hope the clouds and the sun make friends
Come on, cheer up......my little Sun

My Other Brother

When I close the door of my bedroom
My other brother is there
Always smiling back at me
We are the perfect pair

We both have a cheeky angels face
And hair that wont lay down
Happy, sad and playing together
As a cowboy, a spaceman, a clown

Talking the same type of language
That only we understand
Animated, harmonious
With tongues and eyes and hands

If ever I need some company
And no-one has time to spare
I take a look in a nearby mirror
And I know who I'll find there

My other brother is brilliant
On everything we agree
But the most wicked thing about him
Is that my other brother is me!

Need

I dream of a time
not yet born
that
embracing two hearts
two minds
encasing two souls
entwined
brings love.
Full bodied
unlimited.
As unstoppable
as blushing fruit
and a rising need within.

I dream of catching that need
in trembling strands
of faith.
Planting it deep
warm
within your ground.
Nurturing it from
our feet to the clouds.
Caressing
the tender shoots
and deepening roots
until
our eternity blossoms.

Never Ending Memory

There they stood,
frozen in bronze.
Searching for hope
on the metalled field.

There I stood,
frozen in sorrow.
Scratching the history
I'd sealed,
inside a deep ignorance.

There they screamed,
telling me stories.
Casting the sun,
as black at my feet.

There I screamed,
clutching at my drowning ears.
Lowering my eyes
to the street of corporate stone.

There they begged
with supplicant fingers,
for an understanding crust
to fill their famished hearts.

There I begged
my knees to hold
me firm, in this place
of conflicting parts
and personal journeys.

There they promised
themselves and God,
that the world
of scattered seeds
would root and grow.

There I promised
them, my shattered calm
would sow in me,
a never ending memory.

New Light

Now that once pressed noses
have lost their gloom.
New light paints the room.
A spectrum of smiles,
carried on a hopeful breeze.

Now that the sun
has cleaned the sky.
A wondrous blue floats on high.
A sea of dreams,
washed onto a grateful shore.

Now that the splintering wind
has warmed its breath.
New life replaces death.
A patchwork of birth,
stitched onto every acre and bough.

Now that woolly hats and scarves
are asleep again in lavender hollows.
Shorter today's become longer tomorrow's.
A better colour of time,
dressed as rainbow laughter.

Now that spring is here;
all bonnie and brilliant bounce.
We calculate our lives accounts.
A pathway of questions and answers,
leading from darkness to light.

New Year's Cloak

All we do is
stretch our muscles
and bathe our bones

We mash our hands
in creamy hope

All we hope for is
a relaxing thought
and fear of nought

We lose our way
in pictures of soap

All we see is
starry lies
and the reason why

We seal our eyes
and in blindness we vote

All we gain is
a sense of loss
at enormous cost

We forget the fight
in new year's cloak

All we are is
all they tell us
and everything we see

We repeat ourselves
in this ritual joke

Noses

Noses for sniffing
Noses for blows
Noses for picking
When nobody knows
Noses for sneezing
Noses for glows
Noses for smelling
The highs and the lows
Noses for snoring
Noses for spots
Noses for sticking
Into where why and what's
Noses for glasses
Noses for fakes
Noses for boxers
With numerous breaks
Noses for running
Noses for drips
Noses for keeping
The rain off your lips
Noses for nuzzling
Noses for tears
Noses for lovers
To cherish for years

On a Green Bed

On a green bed
Sweet with dust
Two bodies lay
All sweat and lust
Oblivious to
The ones that pass
Their consuming passion
On the grass
Pure intention
Knows not, nor cares
Who looks away
Or stops to stare
Two worlds in love
As clouds melt down
They drift to blue
Without a sound

Party Animal

The music played on.

Some people were dancing,
some stood in groups
glancing over at me;
discussing me.
I knew it had to be me.
I looked away
at the wall;
banging my eyes
on nothing at all.
The blankness echoing
my future acceptance.
But only then after
the ritual repentance.
And I wasn't sure if I could
reconcile my brain
with my actions.
After all,
I was to blame.

Then I realised, why I was there.
"It was me, I did it", I shouted.

That was my speech.
They didn't have to teach me
how to be an island.

Passing Lives of Flowers

Day one:

Tied to iron like a lament strapped down
Tears that fly on hardened ground
Few dreams know the reason why
So many angels stop to cry
Gathered boisterous heads, now show
All passers by, they have to know
That on this spot of modern grief
A knot was sown by grinding teeth.

Day two:

Rain smashed faces like smiling dogs
On guard, lashed, to perform like gods
Souls so distant ignore or sniff
Then pass by quickly, unmoved, stiff
Against emotion, snatched by life
Hardened, immune against advertised strife
A glance, no more as thoughts drift on
Then dirt sticks thicker and beauty's gone.

Day three:

Fractured sunset colours stripped
Of plastic palsy, so ragged clipped
All brain and muscle has squandered time
By throwing gold at fools in line
And as the kennelled worthless sorrow
Disposes of relevance, we're forced to borrow
A hat full of pity when reminded each day
That a droplet of horror has passed by this way.

Day four:

Smoothed to nothing, like air gone blind
Our moist eyes withered; left behind
By to many prayers laid out to rest
We fear our hearts have failed the test
Now all that's left is chewed and dust
A patch, a stain on weed and rust
For the days betray their breathless hope
That a memory shared, will see them cope.

Percussion

Stretching the skin between want need and fear
Tracing a finger from nowhere to here
Breathing your moisture and pulling you near
We enter each corner of passion

Beating a response with a tightness of lips
Gripping the linen damp clinging to hips
Merging our shadows to form an eclipse
We slide to a perfect percussion

Building the rhythm for another refrain
Physical anthems of pleasure and pain
Holding the notes in an endless sustain
We embrace with our futures permission

Picture Perfect Christmas

Expectant souls descend as one
in drifts of sleepy hair and smiles.
Eager for battle to be joined
with glittery warriors of paper and ribbon.
Invading the room, they are captured at once;
the scene is complete; the tableau is set.

Picture perfect,
the artist rests his festive brush
as greens hold reds
and gold greets glistening silvers.
Slivers of brilliant light,
reflecting the day; that moment so right.

A pause; a breath gently held
as glowing eyes, now widening behold
a feast of Christmas hopes and dreams,
displayed wish like, on a heaven sent cloud.
Then urgently bending in playful prayer,
unlived joys are opened and released at last.

Prairie

Dream a blade of grass and
Stretching it for a thousand miles
Float it, becalmed on a
Yellowing ocean, once green with life

Lay on your back, sleeping

Follow its journey from cloud to cloud
From heaven to hell, but
Not in an hour
Not in a fire filled day

Trek through flames, weeping

Breathe deeply into its heart
Holding its infinity
Between finger and thumb
Look hard, now imagine the end

On hands and knees, creeping

Punching the Sun

As eyebrows flutter, sink into the well
A thought of sort of dream emerges
Of wondrous passages filled with light.

Doors ever opening into fields so old
Filled with colours, finally told
Never ending reams of ideas, with
Pinnacles of radiant images
Cascading through eyes sealed tight.

Forging ahead through countless worlds
Into chasms so wide, so high
The tops unreachable, the depths unfathomable
Turning, always churning, finding the way
To new games, old games, good games to play
Losing and winning, no rules or boundaries
Chasing the rainbow though to the end.

Waiting, no, aching for more
No time to think, just drift, race, soar
Rise up, resting on clouds, punching the Sun.

Hot, like the grip of love, pure and sultry
Always expectant, searching, yearning
With gathering darkness, the basket is full
Of unexpected tales of joys and woes
Plunging once more into the opening chapters
Of rhyme and stunning, pin point prose.

Lay back my boy, let it arrive
Like a piercing ray of thought about light
A sabre of visions, no shield can protect.

Bring forth no day, no worldly dawn
Just dreams that work, that happen
Then come true.

Recoil

As each kiss breaks a string
in two, the recoil brings
a piece of you and
puts you in place with
a moment in time, that
once was lost along the line.
A word and deed
that forgot to sing, then
silently died, a whatever thing.
Now, two full hearts
are linked by steel.
A love that's awakened,
and starting to heal.

Reflection

The bright sea gently licked the sand,
loving its softness and compliance.
The sand accepted this love gladly,
as it knew of no other.

The same sea then spat at the rocks,
to tame their jagged views.
The cliffs rejected the waves with a sneer.
A hate reflected.

Rhymeosaurus

Tyrannosaurus
Bloomersaurus
Is it a rocket to the moonosaurus?
Latersaurus
Soonersaurus
Is it a friendly to tunasaurus?
Fastersaurus
Slowersaurus
Is it a coca-colasaurus?
Furthersaurus
Nearersaurus
Is it a cauliflower earosaurus?
Hottersaurus
Coldersaurus
Is it a covered in mouldosaurus?
Fattersaurus
Thinnersaurus
Is it a cold school dinnersaurus?
In thesaurus
Out thesaurus
Is it a troubled by goutosaurus?
Shortersaurus
Longersaurus
Is it a give us a songosaurus?
Eversaurus?
Nerversaurus
It's only a clever rhymosaurus!

Rock n Roll Shower

Standin in the shower on a Monday mornin
My mind's still dreamin and I'm still yawnin
I turn on the water and wait for the warmin
It heats up slowly and then without warnin

I get…
Ice from the showerhead
The dishes are washin
Fire from the showerhead
The toilet's flushin
Frost from the fawcet, is this just a dream
Or a rock n roll shower that I've started to scream

I stagger from the bathroom out of breath
Shoutin down the hall, "I've been boiled to death.
My backside's frozen, and I've no skin left.
Turn off those appliances, I'm gettin kinda stressed."

I've got…
Ice from the showerhead
The clothes are spinnin round
Fire from the showerhead
The chain's bein pulled down
Snow from the mixer tap, is this just a dream
Or a rock n roll shower that I've started to scream

I climb back under and the temperature's climin
Then all of a sudden my cheeks are fryin
My skin's turnin red and I feel like cryin
"If you're aimin to poach me, please stop tryin"

I've got...
Ice from the showerhead
The dishes are washin
Fire from the showerhead
The toilet's flushin
Frost from the fawcet, is this just a dream
Or a rock n roll shower that I've started to scream

Just as I'm relaxin I feel a tap bein turned
And I know that in a second I'm the opposite of burned
I don't want to be a Popsicle, and I think I've learned
I should have a bath instead
Not a...Jumpin jivin thermostatic roller coaster!

Ice from the showerhead
Fire from the showerhead
Fire from the fawcet
Snow from the mixer tap
Deep fryin, deep frozen, lobster boilin,
Goose bumpin Rock n roll shower!!

Rock of Ages

White
Dusty shimmering heat, meets
horizontal bars of coloured sun
The desert is fierce today
Yellow
Nothing moves. Too hot to risk
The breeze from hell tears at the sand
Air has no breath to live
Gold
Silence, save for the dust that flees
past rustling, aching blades
that accusing, point aloft
Orange
No moisture to rot, decompose, just
a crisp death that crumbles and
disappears into the earth
Red
A rock sits, tight with gravity
Surveying the scene. Facing the gravely path
Its journey to life; its prehistoric birth
Brown
Patiently waiting as millennia fall
The rock knows the time is near
No sun could crack its granite purpose
Grey
At first, almost imperceptibly, a tremble
A shiver of relief, a pain's release as
the rock moves; the rock rolls
Silver
Just enough, the new life to reveal
A sparkling addition to the desert's appeal
Smooth, glistening, reflecting the fire
Blue
Staring at its history, the pebble draws breath
Just once, as geology's tale begins again
A very distant destiny. A rock of ages
Black

Rocket to Eternity

Off to the moon
Mars
Jupiter

Ignition on
Flames
Black (oh so black) smoke

Lift off
Crescendo
Needling the clouds

Back on earth
Soiled
Thunder claps

Dressed in mourning
Veils
Hearse of death

Rocket to eternity
Infinity

.

Sad Dad

Have I reached that sad Dad stage?
I think you know what I mean
Do I embarrass you at parties?
Am I so not of your scene?
My birthday tells you I'm forty (plus)
But I know I don't act that old
When I keep pulling faces at all of your mates
I know, I don't need to be told
I pretend I'm fit and good at sports
And run around like a fool
I wear the trendiest clothes sometimes
But don't look the slightest bit cool
I always think a joke I've told
Is so hilariously funny
But you look at me as if to say
Dad, you really are a dummy
I guess what I'm saying is this son
You just wait until you're getting on
When the mind of a child might be still in your head
But his body has shrivelled and gone.

Sandstorm

Ochre burnt by the wind
Blinding uncountable
Unaccountable
Finding a reason.
Any will do

Gritted faces in the gloom
Cheek sucking terrifying
Ever flying
Nerve fucking.
And how

Pounding fists flash tormentors
Soaring indestructible
Roaring at the sun
Light years away.
Dark days ahead

Tracks into the darkness
Grimly leading
Fear feeding
Heading for truth.
Encompassing lies

Grainy wire blanket
Cutting contentment
Breeding resentment
Drilling through men.
Falling as hate

Biting heads stagger
Beaten back
Word hollow
Dry swallow, blame inverted.
Lives diverted

Image engulfed
A suicidal loop of oblivion
On television
Viewer or victim.
It's a choice vacuum

Homeward hearts
Turn eyes to sky
Emotional intersection
Tears without direction.
Lost in the sandstorm

Secret Socks

I'm glad I'm wearing trousers today
That hide the top of my feet
Shorts would blow my cover
No chance then of being discreet
There's something secret in my shoes
That no-one's supposed to see
If anyone asks about them, I'll say
"Oh no they're not with me!"

They'll follow me about at school
It's really not that clever
If my teacher asks, "Did you choose those?"
I'll be quick to report, "No never!"
The enigma in my footwear
Can only be revealed
When I get home each evening
And they can no longer be concealed

So who can I blame for this torture?
That makes me feel so tawdry
It's my Mum that's who, she gets confused
When sorting out the laundry
It's ok for ladies to dress in pink
And in flowery blouses and frocks
But I draw the line at wearing
My sister's Barbie socks.

Secretive Thoughts

Secrets are for the
the people who are
are frightened of the
people who have
are frightened that others

frightened
frightened
secret holders
secrets
want to know.

Senseless

My nostrils fill with hope

My mind fills with imagining

My eyes fill with looking

My skin fills with feeling

My ears fill with hearing

My heart fills with emptiness

Shadow Figures

I see them, corner-like from my eye.
Clouds of shadow figures,
heaped in the darkness
as I drive by.
A languid mixture of shifting shapes,
they pulsate in beats of thickened dance.
Moody in the midnight shadows;
players in an unknown game.

Featureless aggression slides toward me
as I stare, falsely ahead.
A long distance ignorance
that insulates my strategy.
I fly on, in my time machine;
my metallic box of morale.
Glancing looks freeze my head,
as my ears feed me to the ghosts.

I guess at the falling words
and start building the fear.
Then a different direction
brings a dread differed.
My journey is at an end,
as a full stop punctuates the darkness.
I resign my womb; I am born
and it's time to ask the question.

Silent Herald Angel's Ding Dong, While Shepherds See Three Ships Come In.

Silent night, Holy night
A shout is heard, something's not right
"Mum, Mum, I can't get to sleep
I'm hot, I've got tummy ache, my bed's in a heap
Granny's snoring in the room next door
And Jimmy's crying…I can't take any more"

Hark the herald angel's sing
Children are still waiting for Santa to bring
When a tender step on a squeaky stair
Gives up the game, there's someone there
Mum shouts "Back to bed and go to sleep
I don't want to hear another peep"

Ding dong merrily on high
While the night drags on, we wait for the cry
"Is it time, can we get up yet
Has Santa brought my new train set?"
It's hard to know how we'll survive
When Christmas day starts at a quarter to five

While Shepherds watched their flocks by night
The gifts are discovered with obvious delight
"Wow, a Digi-Poke' computer game."
(and an Action Man baddie with a dodgy name)
Pyjamas, pants and pooh bear socks
But best of all……………..the cardboard box

I saw three ships go sailing in
The festive cheer is wearing thin
The turkey's looking very sad
And the Wizard of Oz is driving us mad
Our trouser belts are getting quite tense
And Steve McQueen's jumped his barbed wire fence (again)

Oh come all ye faithful, to
This Christmas time, it's up to you
If you put up with all of its ups and downs
The hangover and the extra pounds
You can give thanks that this winter joy
Comes only once a year........OH BOY!

Smile

A smile can be such a strain
As it binds you to your life
Loosen yourself from this chain
Or it will slice your heart like a knife

Smoking Crows

The gentlemen flapped their jackets
in the charging, woody smoke.
While their chums cackled and cawed,
hopping from ridge to pot
and posing against the cold milky sky.

By a jostle of jabbing feathered elbows,
they to, in turn kippered themselves.
Enjoying the ribald company
on the cracked and blackened rim.
A lofty perch for getting high.

Snoozy Suzy

Snoozy Suzy falls asleep
Anytime anywhere, she can fall at your feet
In the bus queue, in the butchers shop
She'll always catch you on the hop
She'll pass out when it's bright and sunny
It could be raining…that's quite funny
Dropping down, dozing in a stagnant puddle
Her eyes shut tight, her clothes in a muddle
It can be very dangerous, I remember I once saw
Her snoring loudly in an automatic door
Computerised, confused, it swished and whirred
While poor old Suzy never stirred
No-one's sure why she's afflicted so
But it must be terrible when the zeds start to flow
So if you see Suzy lying down
Like having a snooze on the underground
Curled up cosily on a stranger's lap
Or propping up a lamp post, having a nap
Be nice to her and don't play games
Or be cruel by shouting out rude names
Just pass by quietly and she'll recover
Then wander home yawning to her duvet cover

Snorkel

I sit
on my book
with it's ball and chain.
Still here from last week
and next week,
it will be here
for me again.

I watch
the shoppers.
The pretty window hoppers,
the fast food shit wiper
and the hyper children
with their sunken eyes
and Gameboy grips.

I breathe
the same air
as the earnest young men
with aerial hair
and the spacemen who shuffle
their feet on the marble,
and their eyes on the clocks.

I listen
to the trendy old tubbies,
with their blue tooth buddies.
Who think they're fantastic,
dictating to plastic.
They make me feel better
when I talk to myself.

I blaze
with inactivity.
Here amongst the grazers
and the amateur gazers.
I'm the professional,
in my eyrie;
my nylon dugout.

I dream
in my snorkel
and submarine slippers.
Unlike my guests,
the shackled day trippers.
I can shift my thoughts
into those I observe.

I leave
my body,
my forgotten joke life
and move to the exit
mixing nuts with a knife.
Grabbing the handle,
I twist and I'm free.

Snow Storm

The snow storm
had gripped pole and wire,
with frosted stars
so brilliant white
they hurt my eyes.

The tucked and pleated coats
looked sharp and fine,
frozen against the world
of metal and wood
they'd claimed as home.

Later though,
they drooped and sagged,
much poorer made.
The tailor had lost
his needle in the warm wind.

So Grand

Once so grand they stood
Now, so proud they fall

The trees

Each a martyr to its cause
They changed the outline of the horizon
In their own individual way
Shaping, moulding, with gently turning leaves

Now they fall
Just like those leaves
That they nurtured
Each singular, small, but still important moment

Spark

In the dark
we all met
a spark.
Brilliant and beautiful.
So simple;
so tiny.
A single beat,
but bright
enough to light
the world.

In the dark,
we all blinked
at the spark.
Dazzled and delighted.
Bathed in
the joy
that was received
into the nest.
A warm cushion
of love.

In the dark,
we all knew
the spark.
Knew its name, then
planned and plotted
before it died.
With no flame
to guide it
to the mother of lights.
Life itself.

In the dark,
We all wait for
the spark
to strike again.
Hoping and hungry.
Looking
into hearts.
Tearing
them apart.
Searching inside.

Speak to Me

I fail to see,
so speak to me.

What's wrong with me?

Is it to be
my destiny
to fall down free
when each twisted key
is locked in me?

I fail to see,
so speak to me.

Spoons

Gently cupping a breast,
while as spoons, we rest.
Together in our drawer
of soft shawling cotton.
A place where upon
our lives, we hear our hearts.
No closer place on earth
to beat together.
To harmonise in a simple hymn.

A feeling coils around our skin,
as thoughts unwind the touching sin.
So, joined in movement,
as shadows we dance.
Inside and out of our
darkened heat.
Passing a joy to each other;
unwrapped.
Save in a remembered embrace.

Spring Dawn

Deathly silent, the shroud hangs
Midst trees of veiled glass tissue
On high the sun shines glad
That the day lights the issue

A flit, a glide of feathered song
No burden weighs this fellow's purpose
His spirit lofted, giving rein to his tongue
As the air trembles at his gifted prose

The ears that clutch this wind borne lullaby
Freeze, stone like, touched by its magic
Then warmed heart's fly to spread the word
This joyous gift

Spring is here. The truth is right and good
No more frost or snow drifted nights
The sun is re-kindled, rising young once again
And God's garden of life rejoices in its flame

Buds, once shy, discard their cares
Bursting forth this day to a life of warmth
Thrusting heads towards the day
Thankful and tender as love should be

Sunset

Spears of light that pierce through cloud
Paint with colour, a once drab shroud
The gold on green, the bronze on brown
That cuts and stitches a glittering gown

The fingers of wood that plead for more
Their beauty is weak, their purse is poor
Compared with this that cheers our lives
They have no hope, their day life dies

Then just as the pictures paint lies wet
The colours run and fade, not yet
Has a sunset lived for more than a breath
Then is gone from sight, a sad dark death.

That First Flake

Twitching the world's veiled eye,
I gaze tormented, hope like
through a secretive black, as if to pry
under the gathering skirts of night;
searching for that first flake's flight.

All is reported and taken in
from repeated visions of holy words.
The expectation is close to sin.
The child like charm, is now absurd,
like a lesson taught but never heard.

Foolish tricks persist of stares,
beneath that beacon of false joy.
The lamp which illuminates my prayers
is never lost from the mind of a boy,
as winter unwraps his frosty toy.

At last, those jewels of fluttering ice
descend in playful swoops and twists.
Just falling, no more precise.
I cheer, all smiles and fists,
it's snowing, not rain or dreary mists!

I sleep, reassured that the day will dawn
in a brighter, lighter version dressed in white.
No granite face; no damp forlorn.
The world is reborn, at my request.
My vision is here; a balance redressed.

The Alligator

We like to go on the Alligator
My Sister, my Mum and me
We like to laugh on the Alligator
It's exciting and fun, we agree
We choose to go on the Alligator
Every time we go shopping in town
And when we go on the Alligator
We go up…and then we go down

We like to be seen on the Alligator
And there are lots of people like us
It's easy to go on the Alligator
But some people make a big fuss
We like to be cool on the Alligator
The ones that don't use the stairs
We like to cruise on the Alligator
On our own, in groups, or in pairs

We like to go on the Alligator
Jumping on and off is an art
We're happy to go on the Alligator
But some folk don't know where to start
We like to dance on the Alligator
Where as they shuffle and dither like mad
We're cool as ice on the Alligator
The others are wobbly and sad

We like to pose on the Alligator
Grown ups and children can ride
We're quite a smart set on the Alligator
We're accomplished travellers, with pride
We like to call it the Alligator
Though Mum says it's not the right name
But we don't care when we're on the Alligator
Because shopping becomes a great game

The Bridge

Pacing of earth,
pounding the sympathy.
I pause at the bridge
and think of simplicity.
Straight talking sounds
that well up inside of me,
drain through the lives I infest.

Dropping of eyes
into rising obscurity.
I step up to a cloud
and drift to eternity.
Racing the wind
to the final uncertainty.
All of my fears laid to rest.

The Cake

Here we are
two weeks after Christmas
and walking to school.

On top of a cake
freshly made with
flashy ice
we take crispy steps
that follow us along the pavement.

White scatty devils
chase the cars then
settle against the kerbs.

The sun warms us
and the cake fills us
with expectant food;
round and sweet,
complete.

The Fence

In a dream,
I'm looking, from both sides
through a fence.
A mesh of right and wrong.
My purblind eyes dance
from dark to light,
from hard to soft
and back again.
Working out which is which
before jumping over,
or crawling under
into my reflection.
Will I ever wake
from my lover's sleep?
I think not.
So, I'll sit and weep.
While the fence splits my head
and my heart looks on
with a questioning eye.
Looking and waiting,
watching my tears.
Waiting is a curse,
sent by common sense.
I am impatient.

The First Flight

Arrival:

In the grey weathered ranks
we parked our thanks and
paraded to the pick-up point,
in a bleary eyed nervous line.
Behind toughened sheets of expletives
we paused, sheltering in silence
from the wind chilled conversations.
Transported in rattling hollow thoughts
we arrived at blinding echo halls
and checked in our past,
to check out our future.
Our progress monitored
from paper clad coffee,
to the orange tinted dawn.

The First Flight

Departure:

I fought,
but not too valiantly
as the rooftops dropped
and the fields shrank
in the sunrise wash.
I cried
over the tiny forests
of trees and chimneys,
swimming below me
in the misty, hilly haze.
I found
a shoulder and rested there.
Bringing life up to date
with familiar notes
and soft white words.
I soared
above the rocky wool
and saw the home of stars.
It was my home
as I knew it would be.
I closed
my eyes and drifted
in my dreamy bullet
towards the granite land
and home.

The Glove

Do the fingers of the glove,
pointing along the world,
show us the way the traveller went,
or where he'd left his home?

Is it open for a helping hand, or
offering itself for a kiss?

We look down at it
laying there, wearing its frosty coat.
Cold, oh so cold without its partner.
Now lost and unable to pray.

The Hanging Weed Trilogy

The Rope:

Tired of a life that twists and turns
in a tightening tug of war;
the rope hangs listless from the cloud.
Inviting reasons to climb and leave
the world beneath its last, lazy coil.

With no support or steadying rock
to tie itself. The hapless hemp
drift's its knotted end.
Searching between hope and desire;
between unknowing and reckless need.

Step up and grab a length of dreams
But leave the climbing to others
Will the rope support them?

The Hanging Weed Trilogy

The Climbers:

Strung out like a cord of ravenous energy;
all souls of forgotten purpose;
the climbers stagger through our lives,
to claim the latest foothold to deliverance.
A sleeping step on the rope.

Applying rigorous grips, each ascends,
one by one in search of the sky.
Hand over hand, hunger over pain.
This journey's meal though, is never complete.
Each sugared mouthful more bitter than sweet.

The tighter the hold
The more likely the fall
So, wind their souls around a prayer

The Hanging Weed Trilogy

The Fallen:

Below the tattered, climbing fray,
the fallen rest in black and grey.
A twisted tale of shattered lives.
The dropping had been endless;
the impact final. The last big hit!

Each mass of blistered, former life, becomes
a line of black on white, a word in the air.
Then Slithers away in time.
Regenerated as daughters and sons;
washed clean of forgotten sins.

They found the hanging weed
They climbed with ignorance and speed
Then fell, upon a ruthless truth

The Journey is Nothing

Twisted, writhing
like a fallen snake,
it has no pleasure.
Each point of the compass
a screaming head,
deceiving itself.
There are no pearls of wisdom
in this misguided string of souls.

Confused in form and function,
it relentlessly heads
for home comforts.
Those paper sanctuaries
of red wine, blue
towers of sound
and cornered kick boxes.
Sofas so good.

On the bear tracks to salvation,
boxy beast vertebra
snarl, fighting at the lights
with gritted teeth lives
as heart and lungs.
Their exhaustive bullshit
smoking us out and in
and without and within.

Dismembered, fractured
by sharp, grass junctions,
the serpent malfunctions.
Aborted;
pre viability,
as mortgaged mouths open,
to swallow each tired life.
Hi, Honey we're home.

Arrival is everything;
the journey is nothing.

The Last Word

The sting in my tongue
recalls the message, blown
out from dark measures.
Stuck in and twisted, wet
withdrawn from the hurt.
I do not understand, how
the wrong that is done, can
slip along this bloody blade.
Infecting the scratchy blame,
so seeping, it drowns in itself.

When I lay, false sleeping
dragged there by a sigh.
What use are words, of
any length or meaning,
if each is afraid to be tasted last?
My breath is closed, tight
stitched by the sight of grief.
A heart that's been beaten, cut.
As surely as uncertainty must die
we wait for the last word.

The Leaves Have Said Farewell

Having said farewell,
the leaves are gone.
Fluttered at our feet.
Their torment etched
onto the granite field
that carries them off.
Sepia monuments to
a moment in time.

When next the rain falls,
it will dismiss
the memory in our hopeful eyes.
Washing the slate grey.
Cleansing the fallen champions
from our hearts.
An army of faded skeletons,
lain to rest once more.

I knew them once,
like party 'friends'.
They have no names.
But even if they had,
I could not speak them now;
in remembrance.
My voice would crack into a thousand
pieces of winter.

The Lesser Spotted Yum Yum Bird

Imagine if you can dear friend
A bird as big as a house
That looks a bit like a dinosaur
That's been crossed with a quail and a grouse.

Imagine bright green feathers and yes
A crown of razor sharp spikes
It's the Lesser spotted Yum Yum bird
A creature that nobody likes.

(Well do you like the sound of it?)

The Lesser spotted Yum Yum bird
Is terribly, terribly fat
And because it's twenty metres tall
It's feet are ugly and flat.
When it's hungry, it's stomach growls
And you had better run
Because if it catches up to you
It'll bite you on your bum!

(That's it's favourite bit!)

The Lesser spotted Yum Yum bird
Isn't really full of spite
It may not eat you automatically
But if it's ravenous, it might.
You can always tell if it's eying you up
For lunch or tea...not cuddles
Because the dribble from it's gaping beak
Can create enormous puddles.

(That's why it's feet are webbed!)

The Lesser spotted Yum Yum bird
Could gobble you up whole
It doesn't need an invitation
Or a knife and fork and bowl.
It would simply grab you, gulp you, burp and say,
How delightful you had tasted
Then the next time you'd see the sunlight
You'd be on the floor and wasted!

(Mind where you're treading!)

The Lesser spotted Yum Yum bird
Is a bird you'll want to avoid
If you see it, hide, be invisible
It gets hungrier the more it's annoyed.
Don't laugh if you think it looks silly
Or underestimate this nightmarish bird
If you end up as a Yum Yum snack
You're the one that will look quite absurd.

(That'll be the end then!)

The List

Follow the black river,
as it cuts through the heart
of an opening journal.
The forming of a list.

Watch as it flows
through the hollows,
of our heartbreak and tears.
Cleansing the love of fears.

--o--

The city of bridges
and one hundred spires.
A healing adventure
through redundant desires.

A town with a crescent
of gold near the greens.
Where the play was of fiction,
now reality cleans.

A castle with memories
and a history of kings.
An uneasy reunion,
but how our hope sings.

A dance floor of shadows,
that unbalanced scales.
The beginning of rumour,
now the lifting of veils.

On fairways and unfair ways,
past driven by dreams.
A walk clears the air
of imagined extremes.

Artistic impressions,
dumb witnesses all.
Whispered intentions,
now washed from each hall.

A house in the country,
with grounds for deceit.
More love to discover,
a visit complete.

--o--

From source to ocean,
the course of its journey,
in the medium of our space,
is our life.

The black river empties
its guilt into the sea.
Our memories are diluted
and the list is ended.

The Seventh Step

One...two...three...four...five...six...seven.
In unison, the pair descended
into the quiet shadows of the wynd,
which received their whispered treads.
Then, at the seventh step from the top,
they decided to stop
and sat heads together,
jiving lips around their thoughts.
Joining them
in a fingered courtship.

Through the café window
we peered at them; at our past.
Weaving unnecessary threads into their cloth.
The girls though, curtained their hair.
Saving the truth from our eyes;
writing lies for our beliefs.
We understood what we saw
in our darkened rooms.
No point in reaching for the switch,
just to show us the walls.

People attempted to pass them;
threading their lives
through needled looks
and scraping nails.
But the seventh step held them,
suspended in their frosty prison;
unmoveable from invisible ambitions.
Eventually, in time, the veneer restored,
they returned to their shuffling purpose.
Unaware of our watching wish.

Debt paid, we joined the cold air
in searching the granite for the truth.
A hard place to be
for any soft question.
Then lowering ourselves
down the silent steps,
we counted to seven
and sat, pretending we were alive
while the ghosts
paraded before us.

the stranger

quietly in the room
the door closed
a receiving womb
awaiting the baby's birth

who is this man
lying quite still before me
his unfamiliar features
coldly greeting my dampened lips

forgetting the steps to the dance
his name is lost
abandoned in grief

an emotional reunion
with a stranger

the womb dissolves
my back finds the wall
and I slide into tears

The Television's On, But No-one's at Home!

At home in the lounge
It's TV again
His legs ache in protest
His mind lays dormant

The sound and the vision
Wash over him like mud
Oh, how the contrast and the brightness
Tease his eyes with their vain flickering

He wished for an idea
A formation of thought
Pointless, with a brain long drugged
By a box full of bad tricks

The Tune Begins

Eric stopped. Dead in his tracks and listened. The creaking, screaming, pendulous axe had eventually been erased by the distance; diluted by what had been. He sat down on an outcrop of warm transvoid crystal, just formed by the passing infusion and swinging the Yamaha from his tired back, tuned his thoughts to how.

How, in this tortured downward path, he had managed to evade the deaths that should have fallen to him. It was unlike the Yahg to be so careless! Time would tell him, if he ever managed to reach the core, whether his luck would hold out.

The familiar click of a laser finding it's target, tripped his safety to off automatically and snatching the Yamaha up to his shoulder, Eric dispatched a volley of chords into the darkness. Even though he had not slept for nearly seventy two hours, his reflexes were as sharp as when he'd set off three years ago.
"Thank god for herbal tea", he breathed. Relaxing his fingers on the weapons keys.
Far below him, the metallic funk of an Instrum warrior filled the air, as it hit the rocks.

Eric remained motionless for a beat or two, waiting for a bridge of silence to pass. Then, releasing a whisper of fear from his lips, returned to his thoughts.
The responsibility that came with this journey; this eternal search, weighed heavily at times. There was no escape. Everyone back on the surface was relying on him.

He began to think of all those he'd left behind and the beat within his heart slowed. What he really needed now, more than anything, was to know they were safe. He needed another transmission from the composer.

The World in Wood

The world is a wonderful place
The trees flash past our face
The race is on

Who can do better than them?
Nobody can
Who wants to do better than them?
I don't
Who speaks for the trees?
Nobody does
But they want a better say!

Instead of just poking the clouds
With bare prongs of wrath
In winter
Instead of just lightly reaching into the blue
With satin arms of yellow and green
In summer
They want to be heard

But the man disease; the plague
Cuts them down
Strips them of their leafy infinity
Removes their tongues
Silences them forever and
Reforms them for our pleasure.

The Yellow Sea

On one million shores,
the yellow sea washes many lives,
with aching eyes.
Combed by drills and a heavy breeze.
Calmed within harbours
of wood and wire.

Pity the island gorse,
of old green oceans.
Our Father's spring jewels.
Now, reduced to crashing jaundiced waves.
Prickly fists, pounding
the sky stitched mist.

this water

this water is my guardian
it encases and protects
giving energy to my heart
it knows what happens next
it never ever forgets

this water is my partner
it moves like a memory
and understands my needs
it knows my destiny
it gives me dignity

this water is my mother
it cares for every part of me
holding me in a gentle embrace
it knows what has to be
it knows how to set me free

this water is my future
it releases me from pain
carrying my light forward
it cuts a link in the chain
it injects me with life again

Thought Plus Words Equals Deed

Take thought.
The handle of my imagination.
Working through whisky dawns
it leads me down pathways,
pausing at gates to other worlds.
Alternative mysteries.

Take words.
Oh, my painful babies.
It's a wonder they survive
that slashing finger blade.
And the crashing bricks
of fractured themes.

Take deed.
Sloth, nurtured from obscurity.
It rests, cosseted in blanket speak,
while marketeers and money mumblers plot.
Literary alchemists,
turning bread into gold.

Tightrope
(A poem for Tony)

The pavement is your tightrope
As you walk on down the street
Your shoes are polished brightly
Blinding everyone you meet

Image can be deceptive
As the voters now all know
But it's not the cut of your business suit
They'll remember as you go

Your enemies all were sleeping
Until you poked them in the eye
Now they're all awake and declaring war
But you're not the one who'll die

It's the armies of the innocents
In their battle dress and jeans
Who will make that final journey
Down your twisted street of dreams

So, when you fall just remember,
As you approach the final leap
The names of those who fell for you
And the people left to weep

Tiller

Back at sea again.
Adrift between
ports of call.
Carried on tides of
sugared tears
and bitter rage.
I am torn, by a ragged wind
that has no compass.

Unmanned,
the tiller flaps
like a dirty shirt.
Something with a history
of carelessness
and reckless feasts.
I am borne, by a crashing sea
that has no shore.

Taking on water.
Climbing the mast
with a desperate flag.
Searching for a dawn
that scatters the clouds
and smoothes the crests.
I am drawn by a horizon
that has no end.

Time to the Dying

the highest life looks down and beholds
a misty blue, green ball of life
but death is there behind each fold
to creep and slither, to crush and bite

who knows which turn could be the end
the atom of time when nothing is born
the highest life knows the tune
but no warning falls as vision or answered prayer

turning the hands of the miracle clock
to backspace the decades of disservice
might save our souls in minds of fools
but in the meantime our bodies die

when all is lost to further breath
our lungs of poison fail
how long does pain's life live?
tell us now... what time to the dying?

To the Shore

The hot steel ticked, gratefully
sitting on the long baked soil and stone,
as we sneezed the crumbled, blown
history at our excited feet.
Over the fence, we drifted down
through the unfocussed barley heads
with their ripened flecks of grain;
our fingers gently combing
the swaying burnished stems.

(such a fine, golden brush
for tidying away the clouds)

Passing through the gate
hand in hand, spade in bucket
into the lea of the dunes,
a pause caught us in its breath,
before the salty breeze
lured our swimmy steps
up and over the spiky crowns
and down
to the shore.

Touched

A soul passes you by
On its way to the next life
Touches you, heals you
And is gone, to another
Before breath is drawn

True Love Diversion

My heart was spread thin through the air;
trying to cast its beat over a wider world.
But its shadow merely hindered the light.

That was when, in the rude glare of lust, love hid its eyes,
and I saw her everywhere and any time her moves
could be cleared away in remorseful haste.

She had tricked me with a tissue of lies and false promises.
So I gathered my thoughts and my wayward heart
back within a single intention; true love.

Vanity on a Bicycle

Hair brushed
In a rush
Helmet?
Nah!
Hit the road

Bus
Car
Bus shelter
I'm around here somewhere
Taxi
Car
Helter-skelter
Oh, there I am; all ok

Car
No, no a limo
God
I love those tinted windows
Bus
Car
A big estate
Lots of glass. Cheers mate

Taxi
Van
Big bloody white van
People carrier
Phew that's better
All ok?
Yeah, fine
I could use those views all the time

Car
Car
Taxi
Car
Shops soon on the left; not far
Car
Bus
Van, damn!
Plate glass heaven, here I am

Sweetshop
Butcher
Hairdresser
Undertaker
Bookmaker
Family baker
Card shop
Dead stop, it's the lights

4x4 next door
Hair check; looking good
Go
Taxi
Mini bus
Car
Car
Car
Nearly at the office
Bus, you're a star
Van, oh no
Truck
Fuck!

Quick, a short cut, down this alley
Wheelie bins
Metal stairs
Back doors
Despair
I miss glass; I need more
Bin bag
Mirror, laid out with the trash
Can't quite see from here
Ah, there I am...*crash!*

Brick wall

Veneer

Uncharted mountains are stalking the sea
Under the surface of calm silky me
Plant the wood in your mouth and your eyes
Some protection from storms beneath blue cloudless skies
Fighting for peace that supports the old war
Shrouded in dust that once settled the score
Smooth the emotion over rocks in the road
A turbulent bearer of an uneven load
Demolish the idols and fill in the holes
An attraction of opposite high and low poles
Scratch at the polish and crack the veneer
Release all the pressure in a single dry tear.

VPL

Bottoms are tops when they're firm and flat
Bottoms are bottom when they're ugly and fat
But the bottom bottom; the bottom from hell
Is the wobbly bottom with a VPL

Like a sack full of Ferrets, it has a life of its own
And if you wear a short jacket your cover is blown
So please don't bend over with everything saggin'
Just the thought of it's enough to start me gaggin'

If you have to walk away from me, please use reverse
The view if you're short, must be even worse
As the VPL tightens its grip on your bum
The world that follows you feels terribly glum

So off to the boutique with you; to the lingerie rail
But please don't wait 'til the shop has a sale
Fork out for some G's or a new panty girdle
You could even leap over that last fashion hurdle
Go 'au- naturelle' and dispense with your undies
Let your loins feel a breeze – yes, even on Sundays

We Were Christmas

With goodnights passed between us
and droplet lights being done.
We gathered the warm smoked darkness
tight around us and slept
in the folded lives of dreams,
where we paced a floor of stars.
We hoped each would grant a wish
and be waiting at the dawn.
Crisp white. A layer of light.

Woken by a misty windowed glow,
with discarded hours now
scattered in our eyes.
We raised our hearts
and embracing the season,
we danced. All smiling colours,
chosen by God.

In a cloud of song and then
quiet prayer, we played the day
through a forest of thoughts.
We laughed.
We spoke of peace.
We ate and drank.
We gave thanks.
We were Christmas.

Weekend Washing

They arrived,
late on a Friday afternoon.
Two complete sets of clothing
on the washing line.
Dripping.
His and hers, public skin.
No witness,
just wetness.

They stayed,
drying there all weekend.
Then disappeared back to their lives,
first thing
on Monday morning.
Restored to life.
No evidence,
just penitence.

Where Sweet Love Dies

He slid her through his brain
on a bed of lace and tumbled grain.
Her features never left him,
let him rest
in any sleep or wake.
Make no mistake
this was hate.

A reflection one day, heard him say:
Kill her before she kills you with her memories.
He'd turned away.

He brushed her sickened skin
as flat and as thin as sin.
He thought of the key,
rusted and unturned
in the door.
Like any good whore,
she'd been there before.

What was whispered to the world each night
became splintered and daggered in the darkness.
He'd been right.

He planted her satin body down,
on a bed of smoky brown.
He crushed a single red rose
between a finger
and a breath.
It was her death.
It was his

Where Wishes Hide

Christmas Eve, no time to grieve
For a Dad and Mum of a new born son
The brightest light turned out
Their blackest gift unwrapped

Lain to rest at an earthy breast
Quiet and still on St Mary's hill
Gone to Jesus for eternity
To play with angels

-o-

The room is crowded with souls
But we are alone in ours
Sitting opposite each other
Pushing our eyes together
Our hearts spread out on the table

We are unaccustomed brothers
Meeting in a dream
Our conversation begins with
An embrace of uncertain words
Awkward tracks in the dusts of time

Hello, Stephen nice to meet you at last
He shakes my hand and smiles
Yes good, thanks for giving me a call
It's something I had to do, that's all
Somewhere above us, a choir clears its throat

What could you have been, I ask
Anything you wish, he replies
What makes you happy
Anything you wish

Where would you have been
Anywhere you wish
What makes you cry
Anything you wish

Who would you have been
Anyone you wish
What do you love
Everything you wish

-o-

The room has emptied itself
But I remain as a reflection
With just one beating heart
An echo of immortality
Resting within me

I am entrusted
With a life unlived
Where only wishes hide
But as a memory, it is life
I have met Stephen

White Wasps

A blizzard of busy white Wasps.

Blown to a corner of hell, and beyond.

Undecided on solitude or safety,

then descending to a merciless impact.

Dashed to the ground like a virgins veil.

No purity here though,

just real life

painted as fantasy.

Windy Tears

We lived a part of our dream today
Under the sun and small bumpy clouds
Noisy silver crashing constantly at our side
Flickering and tumbling our emotions home

We found part of our love today
Buried amongst the sand and tusky banks
Dusty angels softening our footprints
Those taken and those yet to take

We saw a piece of our future today
Inside our eyes and in our windy tears
Our bodies and souls together, in one direction
Inseparable and indisputable.

Wish
(For Tom)

Great spirit is held in your breath
Your life force cradled in hands of love

Whether by design or accident, it matters not
The world is now a richer place
Where love knows no bounds
Now that it has been found
A place in time, a timeless land
Walking anointed hand in hand

Searching for a meaning
In life's long task
Is just beginning
A journey so full, so extraordinary
That being blessed with a learning mind (no doubt)
Be willing to grasp
All the lessons so tightly, so passionately

So never be still, Tom.
Never relent
Question everything, save for love
Because love is everything
Eternally yours never spent.

Within Me

I found you today, hidden deep inside my heart
I saw you there through my desperate tears
Now you're within me
Breathing new life into me
Can I keep you there, serene and sublime?
A part of my body for all time
I've searched heaven and earth, just for you
God knows I've prayed long enough
Now your soul lies captured, cradled with mine
A heady mix of love and fears

Within me like a passion
Creating day from night
A desert now refashioned
To an oasis filled with light

You could write a book on my body
Your feelings etched under my skin
An episodic replica of my dreams
An illustrated scripture
A picture, drawn on truth
For now I can do nothing but hold you
Feeling the strength of your resolve in my veins
A warmth that embraces and calms us
Protecting our path through the years

Within me like a passion
Creating day from night
A desert now refashioned
To an oasis filled with light

Wood

High as broad will allow.
Embedded in a soil of ideas,
it contemplates the field,
so open, so impossible there.
Crowned with the sky;
running away with the sun.

Limbs could stretch, yes
and roots could carnival deep
in fresh, fertile beds.
How the breeze rustles a sigh,
as impatience stirs the clouds.

A clattering of souls, locked
together in a stagnant dance,
pulls the sticky blood to its feet.
The weight is over
as the sky broods darkly flock.
The chattering is all of freedom;
of new insular lives.

A silent pile of black
becomes a roar of light,
one night, as time inherits motion.
Assisted by a wind of rite.
Bodies wrap around a mission,
as mouths, for too long a foundation,
become feet and walk.

All is mystery and tangled words,
when the life resigned
follows your thoughts.
Occupying the vacant land,
that was once desire.
Arms stretch up for an answer.
All is replanted, but not reborn.

You Bring Tears

Here comes Steven Spielberg's cloud formation
Full of threat and menace
But with a promise of excitement
Hearts beat faster and
Breaths shorten
Brimful and bashing back
With palms spread wide in
Dampened salute
Two storms collide with
Clattering syllables each
More guttural than the last
Heads of thunder roll
As voices charged and full
Pierce the clapping heat
Then, as soon as now is gone
The mood is flattened and
Shoulders buckle to a shivering breast
Avoiding eyes are full and
All nervous glances
As you bring tears

Here comes Sergio Leone's quiet desert
Waiting for the dusty parade
Of threatened clichés
From monochrome hats
Silence bleaches the air as
Words are washed by a cleansing hope

Dried by smiles
Polished by a touch
As muscles lay down
Their weary arms and
Falling pain sighs, ocean deep
A blossom of scented phrases
Fly from sugar lips
Over paragraph pits
When you bring tears

Here come David Lean's epic colours of love
Deep hues of passion
And delicate splashes of pastel perhaps
Poured slickly not sickly
Across a skin tight canvas
A mixture of textured togetherness
Blended
Splendid
Then tattered curtains draw hushed to a close
And gossamer voices sweetly hum
Each muffled by a dream
So fantastic
They appear as
Mountains in the sea
A hazard to the unwary
Because you bring tears

You, Here, Now

Look around at nothing new
Listen for a rewarding view
Not here, not there; empty world
All I need is you, here, now

Dwell on the past, well that's pointless and sad
What's lying ahead; nearly as bad
Isolated, singular, amoebic life? No!
All I need is you, here, now

Hard earning's crop, littered in life
Can't talk, sing or love like a wife
Hold a muscle or two; be so safe
All I need is you, here, now

Discard everything devoid and dark
Remove accessories, useless and stark
Deep breath, JUMP, moment fantastic
All I need is you, here, now!

Just us
You and me
A pair, no cares
Coupled
A duo
Twinned, entwined
The end

Thanks

The publication of this book is the end of one journey and the start of another, possibly longer, voyage into the unknown. To those that have helped me along the road so far, I must say a big thank you. In particular I want to thank, Michael William Molden of Cauliay publishing who has encouraged me to appreciate my own poetry and has given me moral support and guidance since our first meeting. Thank you as well to Bill Kelly of Better Read Books, Ellon for his support of local writers and organising the poetry evenings where Michael and I first met. Thanks also to my wife, Mandy for putting up with the endless evenings of me, constantly glued to the computer; for providing encouragement and positive criticism and for occasionally saying: "Very nice dear, but…"

Thanks finally to my two sons Liam and Joe who have over the years—sometimes quite unknowingly—provided me with the basis for many poems, some of which appear in this book. I love you guys.

29th August 2007